THE RELIGION AND BELIEFS OF ANCIENT INDIA

SUSAN HENNEBERG

ROSEN
PUBLISHING®

New York

Published in 2017 by The Rosen Publishing Group, Inc.
29 East 21st Street, New York, NY 10010

Copyright © 2017 by The Rosen Publishing Group, Inc.

First Edition

Library of Congress Cataloging-in-Publication Data

Names: Henneberg, Susan, author.
Title: The religion and beliefs of ancient India / Susan Henneberg.
Description: First Edition. | New York : Rosen Publishing, 2017. | Series:
Spotlight on the rise and fall of ancient civilizations | Includes
bibliographical references and index.
Identifiers: LCCN 2015050276| ISBN 9781477789407 (library bound) | ISBN
9781477789384 (pbk.) | ISBN 9781477789391 (6-pack)
Subjects: LCSH: India—Religion—Juvenile literature. | India—Religious life
and customs—Juvenile literature.
Classification: LCC BL2001.3 .H46 2016 | DDC 294.0934—dc23
LC record available at http://lccn.loc.gov/2015050276

Manufactured in the United States of America

CONTENTS

THREE ANCIENT RELIGIONS

The Mauryan and Gupta Empires in ancient India lasted from 322 BCE to 540 CE. This period saw the flowering of three important religions. The Hindu religion had evolved a thousand years earlier. Buddhism and Jainism arose only a few hundred years before the first Mauryan ruler.

Hinduism, Buddhism, and Jainism have many beliefs in common with one another. Followers of these religions all believe in reincarnation. They believe that when they die, they will return to life as some other person or animal. They believe in karma, the good or bad acts in their lives that determine in what form they will return. After many cycles of birth and rebirth, they might achieve release from the cycle, which is *moksha*.

The people of these empires used their religious beliefs as guides to how to live their lives. Followers of all three religions believe in ahimsa, which means nonviolence and respect for all living things.

Sculpted figures of various gods decorate temples of the three main religions of Ancient India: Hinduism, Buddhism, and Jainism.

HINDUISM: INDIA'S OLDEST RELIGION

Hinduism is a collection of beliefs and practices that evolved over three thousand years ago. It is the world's oldest religion. Travelers to India gave the word "Hindu" to those who lived in the Indus Valley.

The philosophies and beliefs of Hinduism were passed down orally by members of the Brahmin, or priest class. Called the Vedas, which means "knowledge," the beliefs were written down in Sanskrit, the language of the region.

These texts include directions about holy rituals. They tell stories about the deities. They teach lessons and explain the important values of Hinduism. They stress that Hinduism is a way of life.

The Upanishads are the last sections of the Vedas. In these texts, religious teachers called gurus teach students about the great god Brahma, the Wheel of Life, and how to achieve *moksha*. When followers are released from the cycle of birth, death, and rebirth, they become one with Brahman.

At the heart of Hinduism is the belief in the cycle of life and reincarnation, symbolized by the Wheel of Life.

ANCIENT HINDU TEXTS

The beliefs and values of Hinduism are embedded in the great epic stories of the gods. One of these is the *Ramayana*, written in verse by the poet Valmiki. It tells the story of Rama, the seventh avatar, or human form, of the god Vishnu.

Rama marries the pure and faithful Sita. She is abducted by Ravana, a demon with ten heads and twenty arms. With the help of Hanuman, the leader of the monkey army, Rama and Sita's brother Lakshmana successfully battle to win her back.

The *Mahabharata*, composed between 400 BCE and 200 CE, is the longest epic poem in history. It is a collection of myths, legends, and teachings. The central story is of two royal families who fight each other to see who should be the rightful ruler of the country.

The most popular section of the epic is the Bhagavad Gita, which explains the paths to achieve *moksha*.

The Bhagavad Gita is a dialogue between Krishna and Prince Arjuna. The widely revered deity Krishna is often shown with blue skin and wearing a yellow loincloth, relaxing with his consort Radha.

HINDU DEITIES

The earliest of Hindu sacred writings establish Brahman, the one supreme spirit. Brahman is the source of all existence. Brahman is everywhere and in everything.

Also part of Brahman are the three main gods: Brahma, Vishnu, and Shiva. Together they form a Hindu Trinity.

Brahma is the creator. He is shown with four arms and four faces. He often sits on a swan or lotus flower. His wife is Sarasvati, the goddess of music and learning.

Vishnu is the preserver. He enters the world as an avatar when evil threatens to overcome good. Vishnu has appeared on earth nine times, as both man and animal. His wife is Lakshmi, the goddess of wealth and good luck.

Shiva is the destroyer. Out of destruction, however, comes new life. Shiva has a third eye in his forehead that is usually closed, until he opens it in anger to destroy those who do evil. His wife is Parvati, who is kind and protective.

BRAHMA   VISHNU   SHIVA

The Trimurti or Hindu Trinity.

(See Article Hinduism)

The Hindu Trimurti consists of the gods Brahma, Vishnu, and Shiva, who represent the forces of creation, preservation, and destruction.

STORIES OF THE DEITIES

The stories of the Hindu deities help to teach its values and beliefs. Krishna is a popular god with many worshippers. He is an avatar of Vishnu. He is portrayed as a fat, happy baby. He likes to play harmless pranks. Krishna was raised by cow herders. As a young man, he played a flute to lure away the pretty milkmaids.

Another popular deity is the elephant-headed Ganesha. One story says that Ganesha was created out of clay by Parvati. Shiva beheaded him when he came between them. Shiva then replaced his head with that of an elephant. Hindus pray to Ganesha to remove obstacles in their lives.

The deity Hanuman also has an animal shape. He is called the monkey god. Hanuman is known for his strength, courage, and devotion to Rama. He fought demons and built a bridge over an ocean to rescue Rama's wife, Sita.

The elephant-headed Ganesha is the god of beginnings. Worshippers pray to him at the start of rituals and ceremonies.

FOUR HINDU VARNAS

Hindu society during the ancient period was organized into four main groups of people, called varnas. The highest and most important varna was the Brahmin, the priests and scholars. They chanted the sacred scriptures and were considered closest to God. They became advisers to the kings.

The second varna was the Kshatriya, the group that included soldiers and rulers. They became the kings, major landowners, and military leaders. They were considered the nobility, with the duty of protecting the people.

The third varna was Vaishya, or commoners. They became farmers, traders, and shopkeepers. The lowest varna was the Shudra. They became artisans and laborers. Their duty was to serve the higher varnas.

According to one creation story, the varnas came from Purusha, the first man. When he was sacrificed, the Brahmins came from his mouth, the Kshatriya came from his arms, the Vaishyas from his thighs, and the Shudras from his feet.

Ancient Hindus were separated into four varnas: the priests and scholars, the soldiers and rulers, the commoners, and the artisans and laborers.

LIVING ACCORDING TO DHARMA

All Hindus share various beliefs and goals. An important belief is samsara, the endless cycle of birth, death, and rebirth. When the body dies, the soul, or *atman*, endures and enters a new body.

According to the law of karma, if people behave well, their next life will be better than their previous. Committing violence will result in bad karma, leading to an unfavorable rebirth.

The aim of Hindus is to live their life according to dharma, which is their particular duty in life. They hope to achieve *moksha*, or release from the cycle of rebirth. They will then become united with Brahman.

Many Hindus believe that the greatest dharma is to practice ahimsa, which is respect for all life. They are vegetarians so that animals are not killed for their food. They have reverence for the cow as a representative of the sacredness of all life, including animals.

Hindus revere the cow as a symbol of the sacredness of all living things. Cows are not used as food.

LIVING AND WORSHIPPING AS A HINDU

From the beginning, Hindus have worshipped God as part of their dharma. During the day, they may pray, meditate, recite mantras, and study the sacred writings. Hindu homes usually have small shrines with images of their favorite deities. They may honor them with flowers, candles, and decorations.

Hindus also visit nearby temples, called *mandirs*. During ancient times, the *mandirs* were built of wood and have not survived. Later temples were built of more durable materials. They often have pyramid-shaped roofs to represent the mountains of Hindu legends. They may be decorated with sculptures of the gods.

Inside the *mandirs* are shrines to various gods. Worshippers bring offerings to the gods and pray. They may chant the sacred syllable called aum to focus their thoughts. The temple priest then marks their foreheads with a red dot, called a *bindi*. These marks are signs of the blessings they received.

महाराजा रघु त्रिवेणी तट परग्र

Hindus worship in temples called mandirs, where they receive red dots on their foreheads to symbolize their blessings.

HINDU RITUALS

The sacred Hindu texts identify sixteen events that mark people's growth and development through life. These events are marked by special rituals, called *samskaras*.

For the first *samskara*, prospective parents pray and read sacred texts to their unborn baby. After birth, the parents say prayers and put honey on the baby's tongue. Other *samskaras* celebrate the naming of the baby, first outing, and first solid food.

Boys in high varnas celebrate the tenth *samskara* with sacred threads draped over their left shoulders. They are ready to study the sacred texts.

Weddings have special rituals. The couple places flowers around each other's necks. They make offerings of special food. They then walk seven times around a sacred fire while friends and family recite prayers for future happiness.

The final *samskara* is the cremation after death. If possible, the ashes are scattered in the Ganges River.

Hindu weddings are full of rituals with symbolic meanings. Food, flowers, and fire are all part of the ceremony.

HINDU FESTIVALS

Hindu festivals are based on stories in the sacred texts and have moral and religious meanings. One of the most important festivals is Diwali, the festival of lights, which commemorates the new year. Traditionally, Hindus have sprinkled white rice powder in complex patterns in their doorways. They eat sweets, light lamps, and set off fireworks.

Navratri lasts for nine days in the months of September or October. It is devoted to the goddesses Durga, Lakshmi, and Sarasvati, goddess of the arts. Each night, Hindus visit their *mandir* and dance around the shrine of Durga. They say prayers for health and prosperity.

Holi is the festival that welcomes spring. It honors the legend of Holika, a wicked witch burned in a bonfire when she tried to kill a follower of Krishna. Hindus throw colored powders at each other, sing, and dance to show the mischief and fun of the young Krishna.

Holi is a fun festival for Hindus, when they celebrate the beginning of spring by throwing colorful powders at each other.

BUDDHISM BEGINS IN INDIA

Buddhism began in ancient India in the fifth and sixth centuries BCE. This religion is based on the teachings of the Buddha, who is not a god, but a man who spent his life seeking enlightenment.

Siddhartha Gautama was the wealthy son of a noble. After encountering the three different aspects of human suffering, he gave up his luxurious life. He wandered for the next six years living as an ascetic, a person who practices extreme self-denial. One day, while meditating under a bodhi tree, he became the "enlightened one," or Buddha.

After this experience, the Buddha lived as a monk. He traveled around India teaching the dharma. He taught that each person must find the truth of life for himself or herself.

The Buddha died at age eighty. His followers believe that he achieved final nirvana and escaped the cycle of birth, death, and rebirth.

According to ancient teachings, the Buddha achieved enlightenment after meditating for seven days under the Bodhi Tree.

BUDDHISM EXPANDS DURING THE MAURYAN DYNASTY

Buddhism expanded in India during the Mauryan Empire. The last great Mauryan emperor was Ashoka, who ruled in the third century BCE. This was a time of great religious activity. Buddhism and Jainism were challenging the power of the Hindu Brahmins.

Ashoka had waged war on a neighboring kingdom, and thousands of people were killed. Witnessing the sorrow of his people, Ashoka felt remorse for the deaths. He renounced war and violence and became a follower of the Buddha.

Ashoka himself went about the countryside preaching the dharma. He ordered the inscriptions of Buddhist beliefs on rocks and pillars. To practice ahimsa, he banned hunting and violent sports. He built hospitals, planted trees, and dug wells for water.

In order to spread Buddhism, Ashoka sent Buddhists monks on missions to other kingdoms throughout Asia. After his death, Buddhism declined in India, and Hinduism again became the most prominent religion.

Emperor Ashoka renounced violence and converted to Buddhism after many lives were lost in a war with his enemies. This limestone carving depicts Ashoka lying prostrate before the Buddha.

WHAT IS BUDDHISM?

After his enlightenment, the Buddha taught his first lesson. He drew a wheel on the ground. The wheel showed the endless cycle of life, death, and rebirth. To escape the cycle, people should follow the Middle Path. No one should have too much or too little. By following the Buddha's teachings, one could reach nirvana, a state of perfect peace and happiness.

The Three Jewels of Buddhism are symbols of the path to achieve enlightenment. They are the Buddha himself, the dharma, and the *sangha*, or Buddhist community.

The *sanghas* are made up of monks and nuns. They meditate, study, and teach the dharma. The Buddha taught that there were Four Noble Truths. The first Noble Truth is that suffering exists. Second, the reason for suffering is greed. Third, the way to end suffering is to eliminate people's desire for worldly goods. Fourth, the cure for greed is the Eightfold Path.

The Buddha, depicted as surrounded by monks in this fresco, instructed his followers to live simple lives. Buddhist monks give up their possessions and must beg for their food.

THE EIGHTFOLD PATH TO ENLIGHTENMENT

Every Buddhist tries to follow the eight steps to reaching nirvana. These steps are called the Eightfold Path. A basic step, even before the eight listed steps, is Right Association. One must keep the right company, such as with other seekers of the Middle Way.

The Eight Steps begins with Right Knowledge of the Buddha's teachings. Followers must understand the Four Noble Truths. Having Right Thoughts and Right Speech means being kind and not using angry words or telling lies. Right Action is not harming any person or action.

The fifth step is Right Livelihood. Buddhists should choose occupations that promote well-being and do not make anyone suffer. Right Effort requires thought before action and curbing selfishness. Right Mindfulness calls for self-examination and awareness. One Buddhist text begins, "All we are is a result of what we have thought." Right Concentration is a calm, focused mind.

Buddhists use a wheel to symbolize the Eightfold Path, which is a list of steps outlining the right actions that lead to the final goal of nirvana. The deer reference the deer park in Varanasi where the first sermon was given by the Buddha.

BUDDHIST ART

The earliest Buddhist art never showed images of Buddha. They showed symbols instead. The lotus flower, a wheel, a bodhi tree, and a footprint all represent a part of Buddha's teaching.

Later, statues of Buddha were used to teach important beliefs. Buddha can be shown standing, sitting, or lying on his side.

The sitting Buddha's hand gestures, called mudras, have special meanings. A hand touching the ground is calling the earth to witness. A raised flat palm represents protection. Making a circle with thumb and first finger is teaching the dharma. Buddha is always shown with a jeweled topknot on his head.

After Buddha's death, his followers built stupas, or monuments, to house his ashes and those of important monks. Stupas can also house sacred texts or commemorate special events. The earliest ones were small structures shaped like domes. They are sometimes decorated with symbols of Buddha's life.

The lotus flower grows through murky water to float on the surface of a pond. In Buddhism, it symbolizes spiritual purity.

THE PALI CANON

The Buddha taught for forty-five years after his enlightenment. But he did not write down his lessons. For hundreds of years after his death, his teachings were passed down by word of mouth. Then, in the first century BCE, the Pali Canon was created.

The oldest writings are called the Tipitaka, or Three Baskets. The first basket explains the rules for monks and nuns. The second basket holds the Buddha's teachings. The third discusses the teachings.

The Pali Canon also contains stories of the former lives of the Buddha, called the Jatakas. In these, he appears as a king, an outcast, or a god. Some popular stories use animals as characters. In one story, a golden deer saves a man from drowning. But the man betrays the deer to earn a reward. The nobleness of the deer and the treachery of the man are discovered. The man learns an important lesson about honor and forgiveness.

In one of the stories of the Jakata, a king is introduced to a luxurious palace life with his new queen.

WHAT IS JAINISM?

Jainism is a religion that was founded in the sixth century BCE by Vardhamana Mahavira. Mahavira is believed to be the last of twenty-four Tirthankaras. Also called Jinas, these are perfect human teachers who lived in the distant past. Mahavira's followers founded a community of monks, which grew quickly.

Jains shared some beliefs with Hindus. They believed in the cycle of birth, death, and rebirth. However, Jains disagreed with some of the traditions of Hinduism. They opposed the power and influence of the Brahmin class.

The first Mauryan emperor, Chandragupta Maurya, became a Jain late in his life. He was influenced by a Jain wise man who predicted that India would suffer from a severe famine. When the famine did indeed come, Chandragupta tried to save his people. Unable to relieve their suffering, he fasted to death.

During the Gupta dynasty, the Jains migrated to central and western India.

Mahavira, believed to be the twenty-fourth and last Tirthankara, was given the title "Jina," or "Conqueror."

WHAT DO JAINS BELIEVE?

Jains believe that they should live a life of respect and simplicity. One of the most important beliefs of Jainism is ahimsa. Jain monks wear a face cloth to avoid breathing in and harming insects.

Jains try to follow the Three Jewels. These are Right Knowledge, Right Faith, and Right Conduct. They give up things that are pleasurable to become free from karma. One group of monks, the Digambara, gives up all clothing and walks about naked.

One Jain story teaches respect for different perspectives. Six blind men were asked to figure out what an elephant looked like by feeling different parts of its body. The man who felt the leg said the elephant was like a pillar. The one who felt the tail said an elephant was like a rope, and so on. A wise man explained that they were all right. There are many ways of looking at truth.

Followers of Jainism practice the philosophy of ahimsa, in which they use masks to avoid accidentally breathing in an insect.

JAIN FESTIVALS

Most Jains try to live without becoming attached to material things. Their festivals remind them of their goal of becoming free of the world.

Paryusana is celebrated at the Jain year-end in August. For eight days, Jains try to live like monks. They confess their sins and make peace with their enemies. They fast and recite scriptures. On the last day, they attend their temple for a group confession.

Jains celebrate Karttika at the same time that Hindus celebrate Diwali. They light lamps to honor the nirvana of Mahavira. It marks the end of the rainy season in India, when Jain monks resume their life of wandering.

The festival of Mastakabhisheka is held every twelve years. Jains visit the fifty-six-foot-tall (seventeen-meter-tall) statue of Bahubali, one of the Tirthankaras, in southern India. They anoint his head with water, milk, saffron, and flower petals.

Every twelve years, Jains celebrate the festival of Mahamastakabhisheka, when they anoint statues of Bahubali with water, milk, saffron, and flowers.

GLOSSARY

ahimsa Noninjury.

aum Sacred expression in Hindu worship.

avatar One of various physical forms in which a divine being may appear.

Brahmin Highest or priestly class in traditional Hindu societies.

dharma Person's duty in daily life.

guru Teacher who offers spiritual wisdom and advice.

karma A person's good and bad acts in life, which affect rebirth and the possibility of moksha.

mandir A Hindu temple.

mantras Prayers and sacred phrases.

meditate To relax one's mind and body using a regular program of mental exercise.

moksha Salvation or release from the cycle of birth and rebirth.

nirvana A state where there is no suffering.

reincarnation Rebirth of a dead person's soul in a new body.

samsara Wheel of Life, representing the cycle of birth and rebirth.

samskaras Sixteen rituals that mark important stages in a Hindu's life.

Sanskrit Ancient, sacred language of Hinduism.

varnas Social classes of people according to ancient Hindu tradition.

FOR MORE INFORMATION

Buddha Dharma Education Association
78 Bentley Road, Tullera, via Lismore NSW 2480
Australia
Website: http://www.buddhanet.net
This online library of information about Buddhism offers e-books, web
links, audio downloads, and other resources pertaining to Buddhism
and meditation.

Buddhist Churches of America
1710 Octavia Street
San Francisco, CA 94109
(415) 776-5600
Website: http://buddhistchurchesofamerica.org
This network offers resources and contact information for Buddhist
churches across the United States.

Hindu American Foundation
910 Seventeenth Street NW, Suite 316A
Washington, DC 20006
(202) 223-8222
Website: http://www.hafsite.org
This organization promotes advocacy for Americans of the Hindu faith
and culture.

Institute for World Religions
Berkeley Buddhist Monastery
2304 McKinley Avenue
Berkeley, CA 94703
(510) 848-3440
Website: http://www.berkeleymonastery.org

This monastery is an active spiritual center in the Bay Area. It offers education, information, and recipes for those interested in the Buddhist way.

WEBSITES

Because of the changing nature of Internet links, Rosen Publishing has developed an online list of websites related to the subject of this book. This site is updated regularly. Please use this link to access this list:

http://www.rosenlinks.com/SRFAC/ireli

FOR FURTHER READING

Adams, Simon. *The Story of World Religions*. New York, NY: Rosen Publishing Group, 2012.

Archer, Peter. *Religion 101*. Avon, MA: Adams Media, 2014.

Bankston, John. *Ancient India/Maurya Empire*. Newark, DE: Mitchell Lane Publishers, 2012.

Brodd, Jeffrey. *World Religions: A Voyage of Discovery*. Fourth ed. Winona, MN: St. Mary's Press, 2015.

Cooper, Alison. *Facts About Buddhism*. New York, NY: Rosen Publishing Group, 2011.

Cooper, Alison. *Facts About Hinduism*. New York, NY: Rosen Publishing Group, 2011.

Das, Rasamandala. *The Illustrated Encyclopedia of Hinduism*. London, England: Lorenz Books, 2012.

DK Publishing. *The Religions Book: Big Ideas Simply Explained*. New York, NY: DK Publishing, 2013.

Eck, Diana. *India: A Sacred Geography*. New York, NY: Three Rivers Press, 2012.

Fohr, Sherry. *Jainism: A Guide for the Perplexed*. London, England: Bloomsbury Academic, 2015.

Gyatso, Tenzin (14th Dalai Lama), and Thubten Chodron. *Buddhism: One Teacher, Many Traditions*. Somerville, MA: Wisdom Publications, 2014.

Harris, Ian. *An Illustrated Guide to Buddhism*. London, England: Anness Publishing Ltd., 2011.

Holm, Kirsten. *Everyday Life in Ancient India* (Jr. Graphic Ancient Civilizations). New York, NY: Rosen Publishing Group, 2012.

Lahiri, Nayanjot. *Ashoka in Ancient India*. Cambridge, MA: Harvard University Press, 2015.

Lassieur, Allison. *Ancient India*. New York, NY: Scholastic, 2012.

BIBLIOGRAPHY

Bowker, John. *World Religions: The Great Faiths Explored & Explained.* New York, NY: DK Publishing, 2006.

Bruilly, Elizabeth, Joanne O'Brien, Martin Palmer, and Martin E. Marty. *Religions of the World: The Illustrated Guide to Origins, Beliefs, Traditions & Festivals.* New York, NY: Checkmark Books, 2005.

Clothey, Fred. *Religion in India.* New York, NY: Routledge, 2006.

Doniger, Wendy. *On Hinduism.* Oxford, England: Oxford University Press, 2014.

Keay, John. *India: A History.* New York, NY: HarperCollins, 2000.

The Metropolitan Museum of Art. "Recognizing the Gods." Heilbrunn Timeline of Art History. 2000-2015. Retrieved December 11, 2015 (http://www.metmuseum.org/toah/hd/gods/hd_gods.htm).

Oxtoby, Willard, Roy C. Amore, and Amir Hussain. *World Religions: Eastern Traditions.* Fourth ed. Oxford, England: Oxford University Press, 2014.

Rosinsky, Natalie. *Hinduism* (World Religions). Mankato, MN: Compass Point Books, 2010.

Smithsonian Institution. "Hindu Belief & Practice." Ritual, Religion & Spirituality. 2015. Retrieved December 11, 2015 (http://www.asia.si.edu/explore/indianart/belief.asp).

Wilkins, W. J. *Hindu Gods and Goddesses.* Mineola, NY: Dover Publications, 2003.

INDEX

ABOUT THE AUTHOR

Susan Henneberg holds degrees in English and medieval history from the University of California, Santa Barbara. She has taught literature, writing, and history at the high school and college levels. An author of numerous young adult non-fiction books, she lives in Reno, Nevada.

PHOTO CREDITS